MARCHA CRIANÇA

3º ANO
ENSINO FUNDAMENTAL

LÍNGUA INGLESA

Eliete Canesi Morino

Graduada pela Pontifícia Universidade Católica de São Paulo (PUC-SP)
em Língua e Literatura Inglesa e Tradução e Interpretação.
Especialização em Língua Inglesa pela International Bell School of London.
Pós-graduada em Metodologia da Língua Inglesa pela Faculdade de Tecnologia e Ciência.
Atuou como professora na rede particular de ensino e em projetos comunitários.

Rita Brugin de Faria

Graduada pela Faculdade de Arte Santa Marcelina
e pela Faculdade Paulista de Arte.
Especialização em Língua Inglesa pela International Bell School of London.
Pós-graduada em Metodologia da Língua Inglesa pela Faculdade de Tecnologia e Ciência.
Especialista em alfabetização, atuou como professora e coordenadora
pedagógica nas redes pública e particular de ensino.

editora scipione

editora scipione

Presidência: Mario Ghio Júnior

Direção editorial: Lidiane Vivaldini Olo

Gerência editorial: Viviane Carpegiani

Gestão de área: Tatiany Renó (Anos Iniciais)

Edição: Mariangela Secco (coord.), Ana Lucia Militello

Planejamento e controle de produção: Flávio Matuguma, Juliana Batista, Felipe Nogueira e Juliana Gonçalves

Revisão: Kátia Scaff Marques (coord.), Brenda T. M. Morais, Cláudia Virgílio, Daniela Lima, Malvina Tomáz e Ricardo Miyake

Arte: André Gomes Vitale (ger.), Catherine Saori Ishihara (coord.), Christine Getschko (edição de arte)

Diagramação: Ponto Inicial Design Gráfico

Iconografia e tratamento de imagem: André Gomes Vitale (ger.), Claudia Bertolazzi e Denise Durand Kremer (coord.), Iron Mantovanello (pesquisa), Fernanda Crevin (tratamento de imagens)

Licenciamento de conteúdos de terceiros: Roberta Bento (gerente); Jenis Oh (coord.); Liliane Rodrigues e Flávia Zambon (analistas); Raísa Maris Reina (assist.)

Ilustrações: Fabiana Faiallo (Aberturas de unidade), Ari Nicolosi, Ilustra Cartoon, Marimbando e Sirayama

Design: Gláucia Correa Koller (ger.), Flávia Dutra e Gustavo Vanini (proj. gráfico e capa), Erik Taketa (pós-produção)

Ilustração de capa: Estúdio Luminos

Todos os direitos reservados por Editora Scipione S.A.
Avenida Paulista, 901, 6º andar – Bela Vista
São Paulo – SP – CEP 01310-200
http://www.somoseducacao.com.br

Dados Internacionais de Catalogação na Publicação (CIP)

```
Morino, Eliete Canesi
   Marcha Criança : Língua Inglesa : 1º ao 5º ano /
Eliete Canesi Morino, Rita Brugin. -- 3. ed. -- São
Paulo : Scipione, 2020.
   (Coleção Marcha Criança ; vol. 1 ao 5)

Bibliografia

1. Língua inglesa (Ensino fundamental) - Anos iniciais
I. Título II. Brugin, Rita III. Série
                                        CDD 372.652
20-1102
```

Angélica Ilacqua - Bibliotecária - CRB-8/7057

2020
Código da obra CL 745886
CAE 721143 (AL) / 721144 (PR)
ISBN 9788547403072 (AL)
ISBN 9788547403089 (PR)
3ª edição
1ª impressão
De acordo com a BNCC.

Impressão e acabamento: Corprint

Uma publicação  SOMOS EDUCAÇÃO

Com ilustrações de **Fabiana Faiallo**, seguem abaixo os créditos das fotos utilizadas nas aberturas de Unidade:

UNIDADE 1: **Parede de tijolos:** Dmitry Maltsev/Shutterstock, **Arbusto:** Chansom Pantip/Shutterstock, **Cadeira alta:** Oberonoff/Shutterstock, **Porta:** Vaclav Volrab/Shutterstock, **Copo com suco:** sangsiripech/Shutterstock, **Relógio:** ThavornC/Shutterstock, **Folha de palmeira:** ThavornC/Shutterstock, **Prato com macarrão:** ThavornC/Shutterstock, **Salada:** spaxiax/Shutterstock, **Árvore:** Jan Martin Will/Shutterstock, **Pilha de pratos:** slavapolo/Shutterstock; **Céu:** tj-rabbit/Shutterstock, **Vaso com flores:** Hintau Aliaksei/Shutterstock, **Óculos:** benjamas154/Shutterstock, **Boina:** Djem/Shutterstock, **Vaso com planta:** kvsan/Shutterstock, **Textura de madeira:** primopiano/Shutterstock; **Jarra com suco:** Jiri Hera/Shutterstock.

UNIDADE 2: **Locomotiva:** GE_4530/Shutterstock, **Capacetes:** Chattaphan Sakulthong/Shutterstock, **Motocicleta:** Supertrooper/Shutterstock, **Carro:** Andrey Lobachev/Shutterstock, *Skate:* yurchello108/Shutterstock, **Ônibus:** Regien Paassen/Shutterstock, **Árvores:** kpboonjit/Shutterstock, **Bicicleta:** Gilang Prihardono/Shutterstock, **Avião:** phive/Shutterstock.

UNIDADE 3: **Luminária:** photka/Shutterstock, **Asfalto:** trezvo/Shutterstock, **Trigo:** Big Foot Productions/Shutterstock, **Janela retangular:** goran cakmazovic/Shutterstock, **Grade:** severjn/Shutterstock, **Árvores:** gan chaonan/Shutterstock, **Janela com topo arredondado:** goran cakmazovic/Shutterstock.

UNIDADE 4: **Parede de tijolos:** UvGroup/Shutterstock, **Bola de basquete:** View-point/Shutterstock, **Jogo de damas:** Hurst Photo/Shutterstock, **Tigela azul:** Ratana Prongjai/Shutterstock, **Bola de vôlei:** Aptyp_koK/Shutterstock, **Cachorro:** cynoclub/Shutterstock, **Folha de planta 1:** Africa Studio/Shutterstock, **Cadeira de rodas:** maimu/Shutterstock, **Céu 1:** detchana wangkheeree/Shutterstock, **Folha de planta 2:** studio2013/Shutterstock, **Arbusto:** BK foto/Shutterstock, **Folha de planta 3:** YUTHANA CHORADET NESS/Shutterstock, **Céu 2:** sumroeng chinnapan/Shutterstock, **Mesa:** kibri_ho/Shutterstock, **Textura de madeira:** Sasin Paraksa/Shutterstock, **Tapete:** zef_art/shutterstock.

APRESENTAÇÃO

Querido aluno, querida aluna,

Quanto mais cedo começamos a estudar uma segunda língua, mais simples e fácil é aprendê-la.

Com a coleção **Marcha Criança – Língua Inglesa**, você descobrirá que o inglês já faz parte do dia a dia, e esperamos que você tenha prazer em aprender esse idioma, tão necessário para entender melhor o mundo em que vivemos.

Aqui você encontra um modo divertido de aprender por meio de diversas atividades, como colagens, desenhos, pinturas, dramatizações, jogos, canções e muito mais!

Participe com entusiasmo das aulas e aproveite esta oportunidade que o professor e esta coleção propiciam: aprender inglês de maneira bastante instigante e motivadora.

Good job!

As autoras

Fabiana Faiallo/Arquivo da editora

KNOW YOUR BOOK

Veja a seguir como seu livro está organizado.

UNIT

Seu livro está organizado em quatro unidades temáticas, com aberturas em páginas duplas. Cada unidade tem duas lições. As aberturas de unidade são compostas dos seguintes boxes:

JOIN THE CIRCLE!

Você e os colegas terão a oportunidade de conversar sobre a cena apresentada e a respeito do que já sabem sobre o tema da unidade.

LET'S LEARN!

Aqui você vai encontrar a lista dos conteúdos que serão estudados na unidade.

LISTEN AND SAY

Esta seção tem o propósito de fazer você observar e explorar a cena de abertura da lição. Permite também que você entre em contato com as estruturas que serão trabalhadas e desenvolva as habilidades auditiva e oral.

KEY WORDS

Este boxe apresenta nomes de objetos e de partes da cena de abertura, que serão estudados ao longo da lição.

LANGUAGE TIME

Esta seção traz atividades que vão possibilitar que você explore a língua inglesa de forma simples e natural.

NOW, WE KNOW!

Momento de verificar se os conteúdos foram compreendidos por meio de atividades diversificadas.

LET'S PRACTICE!

Esta seção propõe atividades para reforçar o que foi estudado na lição. Você vai colocar em prática o que aprendeu nas seções anteriores.

IT'S YOUR TURN!

Esta seção propõe atividades procedimentais, experiências ou vivências para você aprender na prática o conteúdo estudado.

TALKING ABOUT...

A seção traz uma seleção de temas para refletir, discutir e aprender mais, capacitando você para atuar no dia a dia com mais consciência!

REVIEW

Esta seção traz atividades de revisão de cada uma das lições.

LET'S PLAY!

Atividades lúdicas para que você aprenda enquanto se diverte!

GLOSSARY

Traz as palavras-chave em inglês estudadas ao longo deste volume, seguidas da tradução em português.

≫ Material complementar ≪

READER

Livro de leitura que acompanha cada volume. A história estimula a imaginação e o conhecimento linguístico, levando você a uma aventura emocionante pelo mundo da literatura.

Quando você encontrar estes ícones, fique atento!

 In pairs    In groups   Say   Stick   Write

 Draw   Circle   Make an **X**    Number   Color

 Dot to dot    Match   Listen

CONTENTS

Siriyama/Arquivo da editora

Siriyama/Arquivo da editora

Siriyama/Arquivo da editora

UNIT 1

FAMILY TIME

Join the Circle!

- Where are they?
- Who are these people?
- What are they doing?

Let's Learn!

- Family relatives
- Demonstrative Pronouns: *This/That*
- Colors
- Time
- Greetings
- What a beautiful day/night!

MY FAMILY

Listen and say

Key Words

1 Look, listen and say.

grandma

sister

father

brother

son

daughter

grandpa

mother

Tetra images RF/Getty Images

mouse

pet

Language Time

1 Stick and say.

2 Listen and complete.

a) Steve is my _____.

b) Annie is my _____.

c) Noah is my _____.

d) Corine is my _____.

e) Ivan is my _____.

f) Lily is my _____.

3 Look at the picture and make an **X**.

a)

This is my cat.

That is my cat.

b)

This is my dog.

That is my dog.

c)

This is my brother, Noah.

That is my brother, Noah.

d)

This is my sister, Lily.

That is my sister, Lily.

Now, We Know!

1 What color is it? Listen and say.

yellow red
orange

blue red
purple

yellow blue
green

white red
pink

black white
gray

Ilustrações: Sirayama/Arquivo da editora

2 Find **ten** colors in the word search.

A	N	O	V	E	M	B	E	R	G
S	A	Y	E	L	L	O	W	B	R
E	O	H	G	P	U	R	P	L	E
P	R	I	B	N	B	N	D	U	E
T	A	T	L	E	R	I	A	E	N
E	N	J	A	N	G	R	A	Y	M
M	G	U	C	A	A	E	R	L	R
B	E	L	K	A	W	H	I	T	E
E	H	Y	M	A	Y	I	G	S	D
P	I	N	K	P	R	I	L	Q	Y

3 Look at the colors. Complete the sentences.

M	M	M	M	M	M
pink	gray	**blue**	**red**	**black**	yellow

a) What color is the ball?

It's ....

b) What color is the dog?

It's ....

c) What color is the cat?

It's ....

d) What color is the toy mouse?

It's ....

e) What color is the flower?

It's ....

Let's Practice!

1 Listen, find the flower and answer.

What color is the flower? It is...

| blue | pink | red | orange | yellow |

2 Listen and number.

3 Read and make an **X**.

Max, the Cat

This is Max.

Max is a beautiful cat.

He is a lovely pet.

Max has a plastic toy.

It's a blue mouse.

Play, Max! Play!

Sirayama/Arquivo da editora

a) Max is a...

☐ dog.   ☐ cat.   ☐ mouse.

b) The cat is a pet. A pet is...

☐ an abandoned animal.   ☐ a domestic animal.   ☐ a wild animal.

c) The pet has a toy. The toy is a...

☐ monkey.   ☐ ball.   ☐ mouse.

d) The mouse is...

☐ yellow.   ☐ red.   ☐ blue.

e) What color is the pet?

☐ Gray.   ☐ White.   ☐ Yellow.

f) Do you have a pet?

☐ Yes, I do.   ☐ No, I don't.

g) If you have a pet, what color is it?

....

....

4 Look at Tom's family tree. How are they related?

daughter	brother	son	sister
grandfathers		grandmothers	

a) Tom is Annie and Steve's ....

b) Lily is Tom's .... Lily is Annie and Steve's

....

c) Noah is Tom's ....

d) Luke and Ivan are Tom's ....

e) Corine and Terry are Tom's ....

Let's Sing!

My Family

Steve is my father.

Annie is my mother.

Lily is my sister.

Noah is my brother.

Corine is my grandma.

Ivan is my grandpa.

Snow is my dog.

Woof, woof...

Snow is my dog!

IT'S TEN O'CLOCK

Listen and say

Key Words

1 Look, listen and say.

moon

rain

lake

rainbow

day

night

Language Time

1 Stick the pictures and say.

day	night	lake
sea	rain	rainbow
sky	stars	moon
sun	clouds	beach
flower	tree	water

2 Unscramble and write.

a) kys: ....

b) oonm: ....

c) retwa: ....

d) ightn: ....

e) kela: ....

f) yad: ....

g) niar: ....

h) wobniar: ....

3 Match and say the time.

What time is it?

It's one o'clock.

What time is it?

It's two o'clock.

It's five o'clock.

It's three o'clock.

It's one o'clock.

It's ten o'clock.

It's eight o'clock.

Now, We Know!

1 Complete and draw the clock hands.

| What time is it? |

a) It's .... o'clock.

b) It's .... o'clock.

c) It's

....

d) It's

....

e) It's

....

f) It's

....

2 Listen and number the pictures.

Ilustrações: Sirayama/ Arquivo da editora

3 Color the rainbow.

1 red	2 orange	3 yellow	4 green	5 blue	6 indigo	7 violet

Ilustrações: Sirayama/ Arquivo da editora

Let's Practice!

1 Word search. Circle the words.

| day | night | sun | moon | rain |
| beach | sky | sea | star | water |

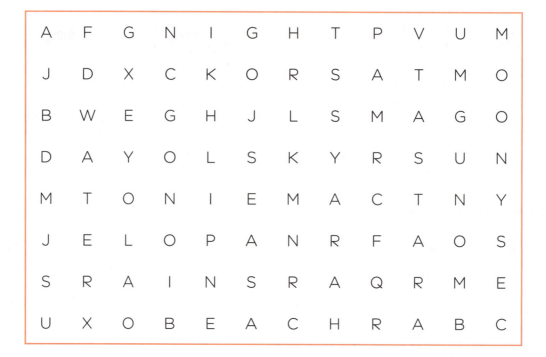

A	F	G	N	I	G	H	T	P	V	U	M
J	D	X	C	K	O	R	S	A	T	M	O
B	W	E	G	H	J	L	S	M	A	G	O
D	A	Y	O	L	S	K	Y	R	S	U	N
M	T	O	N	I	E	M	A	C	T	N	Y
J	E	L	O	P	A	N	R	F	A	O	S
S	R	A	I	N	S	R	A	Q	R	M	E
U	X	O	B	E	A	C	H	R	A	B	C

2 Write the next word.

a) sundaynightsundaynightsundaynightsundaynightsunday

....

b) moonmoonrainmoonmoonrainmoonmoonrainmoonmoon

....

c) beachbeachskyskybeachbeachskyskybeachbeachsky

....

d) seastarstarseastarstarseastarstarseastarstarseastarstar

....

3 Listen and draw the missing clock hands. Then, write the sentences.

(11)

What time is it?

a)

....

b)

....

c)

....

d)

....

e)

....

f)

....

4 Read and make an **X**.

A Beautiful Day!

Morning, morning,

What a beautiful morning!

The sun is shining.

The sky is blue, the birds are on the air and there are white clouds too.

Green trees to complete the colorful picture.

It is a beautiful day! Yes, I love nature!

Felix Wise/Shutterstock

a) The clouds are... ☐ blue. ☐ white.

b) The sky is... ☐ blue. ☐ white.

c) The trees are... ☐ blue. ☐ green.

d) It is a beautiful... ☐ night. ☐ day.

5 Read and complete.

A Beautiful Night!

Good evening!

Welcome the moon and the stars in the sky!

It is such a wonderful night! That simply looking at the sky can make me cry!

Yes, it is! So, I say bye-bye.

Good night. I prefer to dream not to cry.

Klagyivik Viktor/Shutterstock

a) The night is b............................!

b) The m............................ is round and white.

c) The stars are w.............................

d) The s............................ is dark blue.

6 Let's make a clock! Stick, write and say.

Ilustrações: Sirayama/Arquivo da editora

Let's Sing!

Tick-tock

(12)

Tick-tock, tick-tock,

It's seven o'clock.

Tick-tock, tick-tock,

It's time to sing a rock.

Tick-tock, tick-tock,

It's ten o'clock.

Tick-tock, tick-tock,

It's time to sleep a lot.

TALKING ABOUT...

Respect Elderly People

- What do these photos represent?

- Do you spend quality time with your grandparents or older people? Explain.

Digital Vision/Getty Images

E+/Getty Images

E+/Getty Images

Ilustrações: Sirayama/Arquivo da editora

1 What can you do to show respect to grandparents and senior citizens in general? Write **T** (true) or **F** (false).

a) Spend time with them. ☐

b) Do not listen to their stories. ☐

c) Be polite. ☐

d) Ignore their advice. ☐

e) Eat together. ☐

f) Call them. ☐

g) Tell them you appreciate and respect them. ☐

h) Visit senior living communities. ☐

2 Draw an activity you do with one of your grandparents.

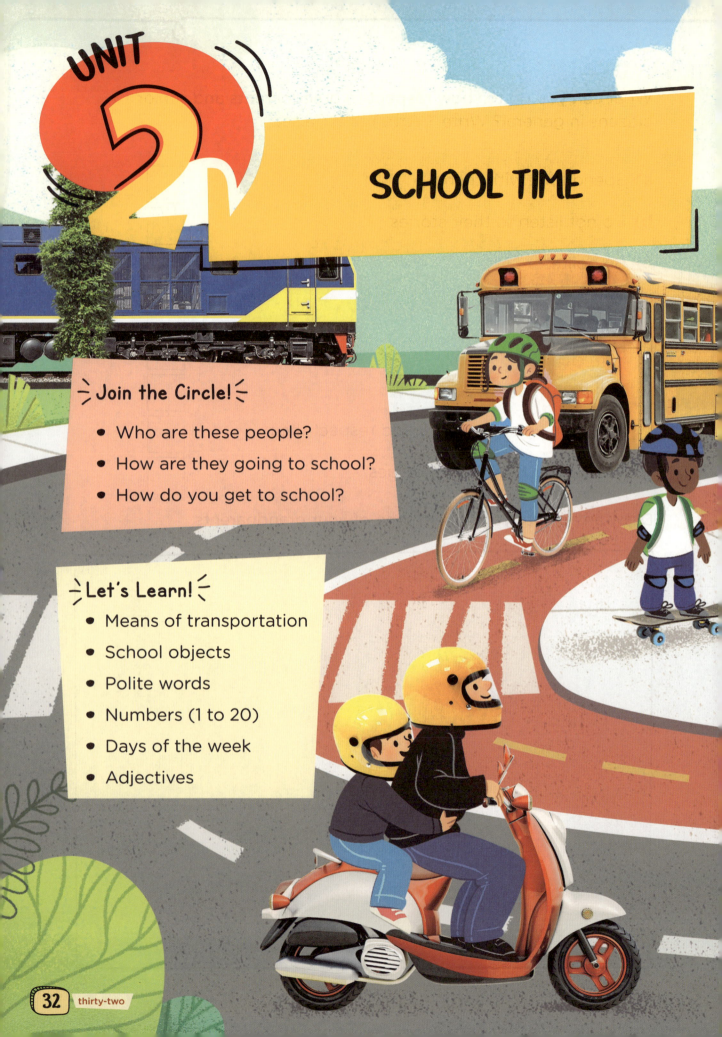

UNIT 2

SCHOOL TIME

Join the Circle!

- Who are these people?
- How are they going to school?
- How do you get to school?

Let's Learn!

- Means of transportation
- School objects
- Polite words
- Numbers (1 to 20)
- Days of the week
- Adjectives

SCHOOL

LESSON 3

A SPECIAL DAY AT SCHOOL

Key Words

1 Look, listen and say.

school bus

rollerblades

skateboard

subway

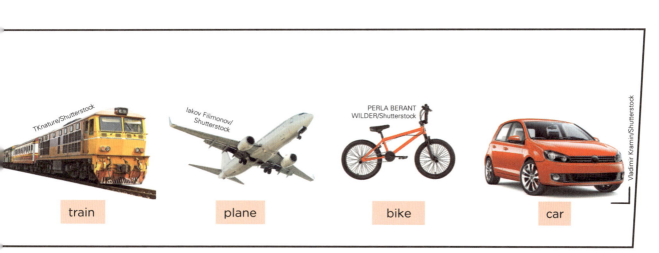

train

plane

bike

car

Language Time

1 Listen, stick and say.

school bus

Verko_o/Shutterstock

car

inkwellapp/Shutterstock

bike

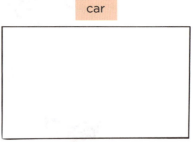

rollerblades

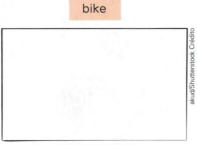

akud/Shutterstock Crédito

skateboard

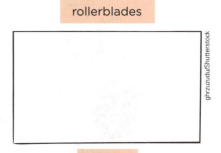

ghrzuzudu/Shutterstock

plane

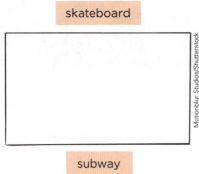

Motionblur Studios/Shutterstock

subway

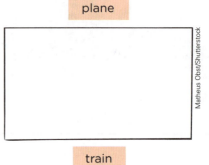

Matheus Obst/Shutterstock

train

2 Let's count.

1	2	3	4	5	6	7	8	9	10	11	12
one	two	three	four	five	six	seven	eight	nine	ten	eleven	twelve

13	14	15	16	17	18	19	20
thirteen	fourteen	fifteen	sixteen	seventeen	eighteen	nineteen	twenty

3 Complete the dialog and say.

| **What is your name?** | **My name is** | **Hello!** |

OLÁ!

SANDRA.

4 What day is today? Say it.

Today is **Sunday**.

Today is **Monday**.

Today is **Tuesday**.

Today is **Wednesday**.

Today is **Thursday**.

Today is **Friday**.

Today is **Saturday**.

Now, We Know!

1 Complete the sentences using the words from the box.

| school bus | skateboard | bike | subway |

a)

This is a ....

b)

This is a ....

c)

This is a ....

d)

This is a ....

2 Write the missing numbers.

one / .... / three / four / five / .... /

seven / .... / nine / ten / .... /

.... / thirteen / fourteen / .... /

sixteen / .... / eighteen / .... / twenty

3 Read and complete.

a)

Today is **Sunday.**

b)

Today is ....

c)

Today is ....

d)

Today is ....

e)

Today is ....

f)

Today is ....

g)

Ilustrações: Sirayama/ Arquivo da editora

Today is ....

Let's Practice!

1 Find and circle the words. Then write them under the pictures.

ONETWOTHREEPLANENINEFIFTEENCARBIKESIXROLLERBLADESCHOOLBUSFOURSKATEBOARDBALLTRAINSUBWAYTWENTY

a)

15

....

b)

....

c)

....

d)

20

....

e)

....

Ilustrações: IlustraCartoon/
Arquivo da editora

TP71/
Shutterstock

2 Listen and act out.

3 Listen, draw and write about Emily.

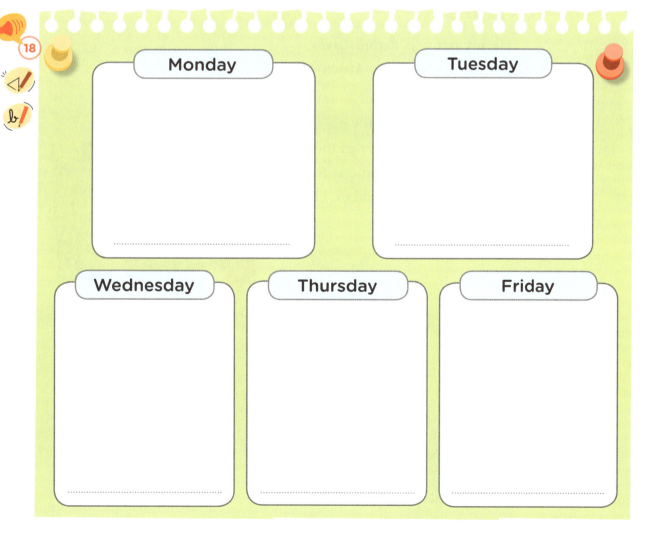

4 Read Esther's personal information and answer true (**T**) or false (**F**).

First name: Esther

Full name: Esther Laye Oni

Nickname: Essie

Country: Nigeria

Date of birth: Nov. 11th

Age: 10 years old

Pet: a dog

Pet's name: Karu

Hi, my name is Esther Laye Oni. I'm from Nigeria, in Africa. I'm Nigerian.

My family is small. It's me, my mother, my father and my grandpa. I have an old dog. Its name is Karu. My date of birth is November 11th. I'm 10 years old.

a) The girl doesn't like her new school.

b) The girl's name is Esther Oni.

c) The girl is from Nigeria.

d) The girl has a cat.

5 Write your personal profile.

Let's Sing!

Ten Ice Creams for Me

19

One, two, three,

One, two, three,

Four, five, six,

Four, five, six,

Seven, eight, nine,

Seven, eight, nine,

Ten ice creams for me,

Ten ice creams for me.

naluwan/Shutterstock

BE NICE!

Listen and say

20

Key Words

1 Look, listen and say.

21

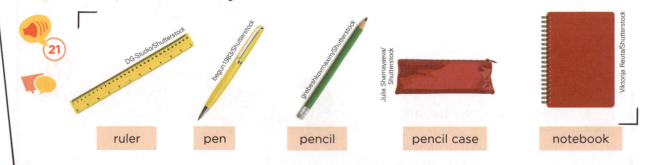

ruler   pen   pencil   pencil case   notebook

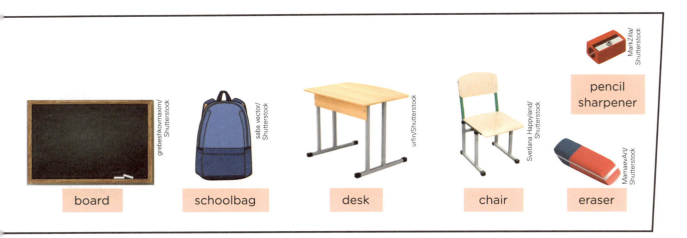

board

schoolbag

desk

chair

eraser

pencil sharpener

Language Time

1 Listen, point and say.

22

notebook

desk

pencil case

ruler

pencil

schoolbag

eraser

pencil sharpener

pen

chair

board

Régua: E._Vector/Shutterstock; lousa: Omeris/Shutterstock; caneta: Pixel Embargo/Shutterstock; carteira: Edilus/Shutterstock; cadeira: Codrut Crososchi/Shutterstock; estojo: Anatolir/Shutterstock; caderno: hasan kurt/Shutterstock; apontador: Laurentiu Timplaru/Shutterstock; mochila: sdp_creations/Shutterstock; lápis: Intellson/Shutterstock; borracha: pear worapan/Shutterstock

2 Look and say.

a **short** girl

a **tall** girl

a **big** sandwich

a **small** sandwich

a **beautiful** schoolbag

an **ugly** schoolbag

an **old** car

a **new** car

Ilustrações: AM Studio/Arquivo da editora

Now, We Know!

1 Write the name of the school objects.

a)

DU Srki/ Shutterstock

desk

b)

3DMAVR/Shutterstock

....

c)

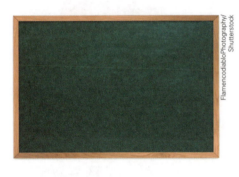

FlamencodiabloPhotography/ Shutterstock

....

d)

sliplee/Shutterstock

....

e)

Mahathaniyasoporn/Shutterstock

....

f)

Svetlana Happyland/ Shutterstock

....

g)

Anton Starikov/Shutterstock

....

2 Write the correct sentence.

My bike is small.   /   What a beautiful schoolbag!

This ball is big.   /   My father is tall.

Ilustrações: AMj Studio/Arquivo da editora

3 Find and circle the polite words.

Please	Sorry	Thanks	Welcome

O	I	T	A	C	Y	M	V	L	G
W	P	L	H	M	F	T	W	B	J
D	L	Q	Y	A	Z	X	N	A	Z
K	E	Y	T	H	N	V	W	N	I
Z	A	B	U	S	Q	K	R	P	X
G	S	O	R	R	Y	J	S	U	D
N	E	F	W	E	L	C	O	M	E

Let's Practice!

1 Listen, circle and say.

a)

b)

c)

d)

e)

2 Listen and number the pictures.

3 Complete the dialog and act out.

please	welcome	thanks	sorry

..................., WRITE YOUR HOMEWORK PAGES!

..................., TEACHER, I CAN'T FIND MY PENCIL!

HERE IT IS!

...................!

HOMEWORK PAGES 89 AND 90

HOMEWORK PAGES 89 AND 90

YOU ARE ....!

Ilustrações: AM| Studio/Arquivo da editora

4 Read the text.

Date: 04/28

Homework

Subject: English
In the notebook, do activities 4, 5 and 6
from the book, page 13.
Deadline: Monday (May 3rd)

5 Read and make an **X**.

a) What is the homework subject?

 ☐

 ☐

b) What items are used to do the homework?

 ☐

 ☐

c) When is the homework deadline?

June				
Monday	Tuesday	Wednesday	Thursday	Friday
⑤	6	7	8	9	☐

May				
Monday	Tuesday	Wednesday	Thursday	Friday
③	4	5	6	7	☐

6 Now, write a note about your homework.

Date: ....

Homework

Subject: ....

....

Deadline: .... (..............................)

🎵 Let's Sing!

How Are You?

25

My friend Carol,	I'm fine, thank you.
My friend Carol,	I'm fine, thank you.
How are you?	And how are you?
How are you?	And how are you?

stockfour/Shutterstock

IT'S YOUR TURN!

linlingtsyr/Shutterstock

Mobility

In groups, follow the steps below to create a model about means of transportation.

YOU NEED:

- small empty cardboard boxes from packaging

- clothing buttons to be used as vehicle wheels

- laminated paper for the glass

- pieces of thin wire

- blue paper for the water

- colored cardboard

- white glue
- scissors
- ruler
- colored pens

- colored crepe paper to create trees and a garden

- a piece of cardboard for the base

- miniatures of trees, cars, dolls and other objects to compose the scenery

- wooden barbecue sticks to create structures such as trees, lamp posts, traffic lights etc.

1) Pick up all the boxes. Cover them with colored paper. And draw the details like doors, windows etc.

2) Draw the streets on the cardboard base, cover it with colored paper or color it.

3) Use blue paper to represent the sea and the sky.

Ilustra Cartoon/Arquivo da editora

4) Draw the streets on the cardboard base, cover it with colored paper or paint it. Use crepe paper to create grass, trees etc..

5) Decorate it with the buildings and the means of transportation according to the scenes: car, bus, motorcycle, bike, plane, helicopter, truck, school bus, skate, scooter, plane, subway, etc.

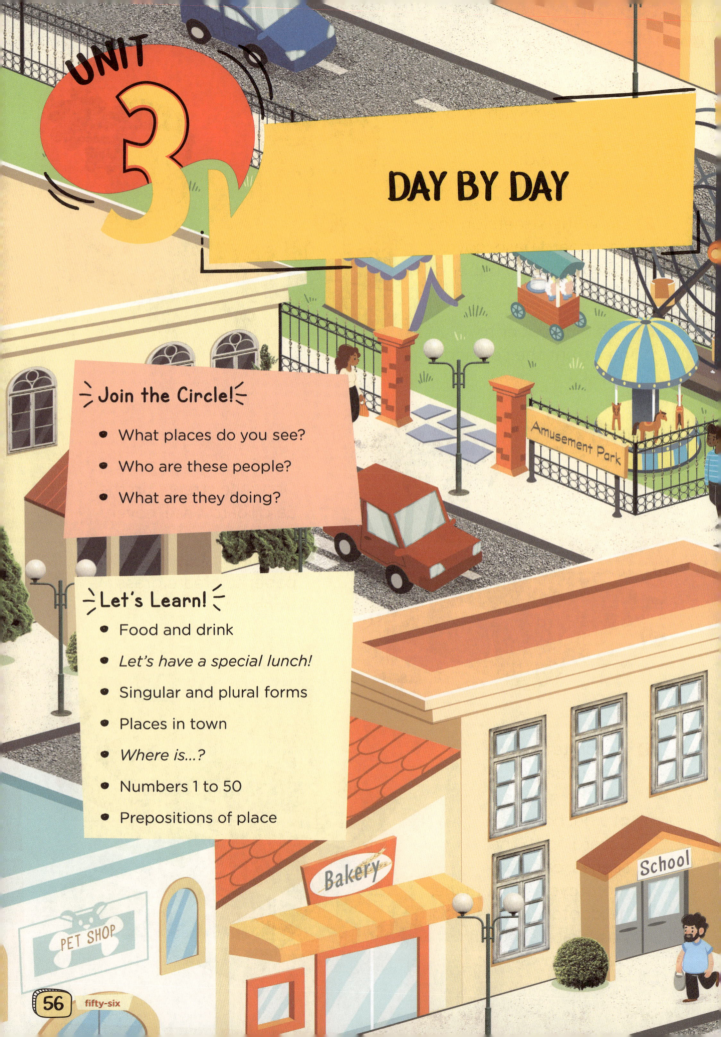

UNIT 3

DAY BY DAY

Join the Circle!

- What places do you see?
- Who are these people?
- What are they doing?

Let's Learn!

- Food and drink
- *Let's have a special lunch!*
- Singular and plural forms
- Places in town
- *Where is...?*
- Numbers 1 to 50
- Prepositions of place

DRUGSTORE

SPORTS CLUB

MOVIE THEATER

Fabiana Faiallo/Arquivo da editora

IT'S TIME FOR LUNCH!

Listen and say

TODAY IS SUNDAY! LET'S HAVE A SPECIAL LUNCH!

MR. SMITH, FOR ME, SOME SALAD, CHICKEN AND LEMONADE, PLEASE.

Key Words

1 Look, listen and say.

| salad | ham and cheese sandwich | tomato | meat | sausages |

Ilustrações: Ilustra Cartoon/Arquivo da editora

To learn more

In countries like Canada, Australia, England and the United States, lunch is a light meal, especially one taken in the middle of the day, between breakfast and dinner. In general, people have sandwiches, hamburgers, French fries, pies, salads and fruits for lunch.

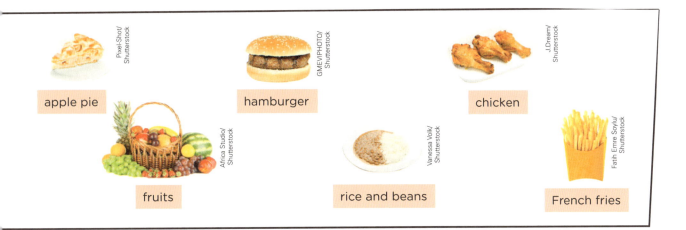

apple pie — Pixel-Shot/Shutterstock

hamburger — GMEVIPHOTO/Shutterstock

chicken — J.Dream/Shutterstock

fruits — Africa Studio/Shutterstock

rice and beans — Vanessa Volk/Shutterstock

French fries — Fatih Emre Soylu/Shutterstock

Language Time

Singular and Plural Forms	
Singular	Plural
apple	apple**s**
sausage	sausage**s**
sandwich	sandwich**es**

1 Listen and draw.

28

a)

one apple	two apples

b)

one orange	three oranges

c)

one tomato	four tomatoes

2 Look and make an **X**.

a)

Horus2017/Shutterstock

☐ sandwich

☐ sandwiches

b)

robertsre/Shutterstock

☐ apple pie

☐ apple pies

c)

Angelina Babii/Shutterstock

☐ tomato

☐ tomatoes

d)

PaulPaladin/Shutterstock

☐ apple

☐ apples

3 Listen, point and say.

(29)

1 one	14 fourteen	27 twenty-seven	39 thirty-nine
2 two	15 fifteen	28 twenty-eight	40 forty
3 three	16 sixteen	29 twenty-nine	41 forty-one
4 four	17 seventeen	30 thirty	42 forty-two
5 five	18 eighteen	31 thirty-one	43 forty-three
6 six	19 nineteen	32 thirty-two	44 forty-four
7 seven	20 twenty	33 thirty-three	45 forty-five
8 eight	21 twenty-one	34 thirty-four	46 forty-six
9 nine	22 twenty-two	35 thirty-five	47 forty-seven
10 ten	23 twenty-three	36 thirty-six	48 forty-eight
11 eleven	24 twenty-four	37 thirty-seven	49 forty-nine
12 twelve	25 twenty-five	38 thirty-eight	50 fifty
13 thirteen	26 twenty-six		

Now, We Know!

1 Look and unscramble the letters.

a) stuirf

monticello/Shutterstock

b) ecri and ebans

iStockphoto/Getty Images

....

....

c) eatm

Gregory Gerber/Shutterstock

d) esmatoto

Wirestock Images/Shutterstock

e) delenamo

Beautyandsoulfood/Shutterstock

....

....

....

2 Circle the odd word.

a) lemonade   forty-two   hamburger   chicken   meat

b) thirty-one   thirty-five   twenty   thirty-nine   ham

c) fifty   cheese   eleven   twenty-one   forty-three

d) lemonade   thirty-four   twenty-five   forty-eight   fifty

e) sandwich   apples   fruit   thirteen   meat

f) chicken   ten   twenty-four   fifty   five

3 Word search.

cheese   sandwiches   orange juice   meat
sausages   apple pie   fruit   ham   egg
chicken   hamburger   lemonade   salad

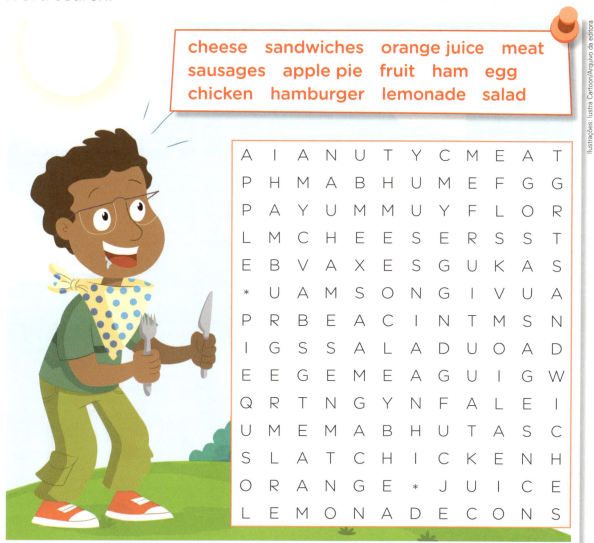

```
A  I  A  N  U  T  Y  C  M  E  A  T
P  H  M  A  B  H  U  M  E  F  G  G
P  A  Y  U  M  M  U  Y  F  L  O  R
L  M  C  H  E  E  S  E  R  S  S  T
E  B  V  A  X  E  S  G  U  K  A  S
*  U  A  M  S  O  N  G  I  V  U  A
P  R  B  E  A  C  I  N  T  M  S  N
I  G  S  S  A  L  A  D  U  O  A  D
E  E  G  E  M  E  A  G  U  I  G  W
Q  R  T  N  G  Y  N  F  A  L  E  I
U  M  E  M  A  B  H  U  T  A  S  C
S  L  A  T  C  H  I  C  K  E  N  H
O  R  A  N  G  E  *  J  U  I  C  E
L  E  M  O  N  A  D  E  C  O  N  S
```

Ilustrações: Iustra Cartoon/Arquivo da editora

4 Read and match the food and drink the boys are eating.

 What do you have for lunch?

I HAVE CHICKEN, SOME SALAD AND LEMONADE FOR LUNCH.

I HAVE MEAT, AN EGG AND SOME ORANGE JUICE FOR LUNCH.

Let's Practice!

1 Quiz: What do you have for lunch?

meat	apple pie	fruits	salad	bread	ice cream
sausages	ham	egg	sandwich		hamburger
milk	cheese	lemonade	orange juice		chicken

I have...

2 Mark **true** or **false**. Talk to a classmate.

a) Milk, fruit and French fries are considered healthy food.

[ ] TRUE   [ ] FALSE

b) French fries and hamburgers are considered junk food.

[ ] TRUE   [ ] FALSE

c) Healthy food is good for our body.

[ ] TRUE   [ ] FALSE

d) Junk or unhealthy food is not good for your body.

[ ] TRUE   [ ] FALSE

e) Chicken, rice, beans and fruit are considered healthy food.

[ ] TRUE   [ ] FALSE

3 List four of your favorite food in the correct column.

Healthy food	Junk or unhealthy food
1 _____	1 _____
2 _____	2 _____
3 _____	3 _____
4 _____	4 _____

4 Read the text.

5 Read and answer YES or NO.

a) A shopping list is a list of items we need to buy.

☐ YES   ☐ NO

b) Based on Bob's shopping list, he needs to buy apples, chicken, cookies and sausages.

☐ YES   ☐ NO

6   Make an **X**. Talk to your classmates about Bob's shopping list.

a) What items on the list are healthy?

☐ Apples.   ☐ Chicken.   ☐ Eggs.   ☐ Sausages.

b) What items on the list are not healthy?

☐ Milk.   ☐ Chicken.   ☐ Eggs.   ☐ Sausages.

c) Are there eight items on Bob's shopping list?

☐ Yes.   ☐ No.

♪ Let's Sing!

Apple Juice

Here's your apple juice,

Drink it down, drink it down.

Here's your apple juice,

Drink it down, drink it down.

Here's your apple juice,

May you put it to good use.

Drink it down, drink it down, drink it down.

Apple juice! Apple juice!

Apple juice! Apple juice!

Drink it right on down.

I'm saying

Apple juice! Apple juice!

Apple juice! Apple juice!

Drink it right on down.

Tania Kolinko/Shutterstock

PLACES IN THE CITY

Listen and say

Key Words

1 Look, listen and say.

amusement park

movie theater

theater

bakery

drugstore

museum

pet shop

restaurant

Language Time

Prepositions of Place

Between
The bakery is **between** the bank and the supermarket.

Next to
The movie theater is **next to** the museum.

In front of
The pet shop is **in front of** the shopping mall.

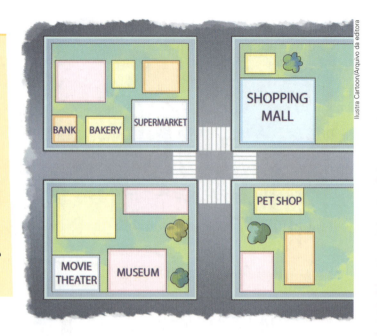

1 Look, write and say.

| in front of | next to | between |

Where is the...?

a) The supermarket is

....

the movie theater.

b) The museum is

....

the restaurant and the

supermarket.

c) The restaurant is

....

the museum.

2 Read and answer.

a)

What is this?

It is a ....

b)

What is this?

It is a ....

c)

What is this?

It is a ....

d)

What is this?

It is a ....

Now, We Know!

1 Listen and number.

a)

b)

c)

d)

2 Unscramble to form sentences.

a) next to / the / school / supermarket / is / the /.

....

....

b) in front of / is / the / amusement park / museum / the /.

....

....

c) and / movie theater / is / the / drugstore / the / between / bank / the /.

....

....

3 Look at the map. Make an **X** in the correct alternative.

a) The school is next to the museum. ☐

The school is in front of the movie theater. ☐

b) The hospital is next to the zoo. ☐

The hospital is in front of the zoo. ☐

c) The supermarket is next to the park. ☐

The supermarket is in front of the park. ☐

d) The museum is in front of the airport. ☐

The museum is between the school and the police station. ☐

Let's Practice!

1 Read, write and talk.

LOOK AT MY PICTURES, MARY!

OH, I LOVE PICTURES!

THIS IS MY FATHER. HE IS AT THE MUSEUM.

AND THIS IS MY MOTHER. SHE IS AT THE MOVIE THEATER.

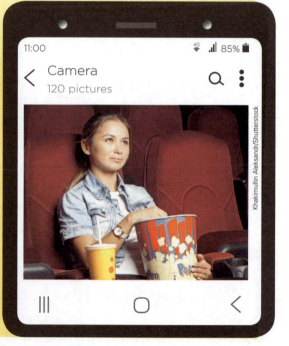

I'M AT .... !

2 Listen, draw and write.

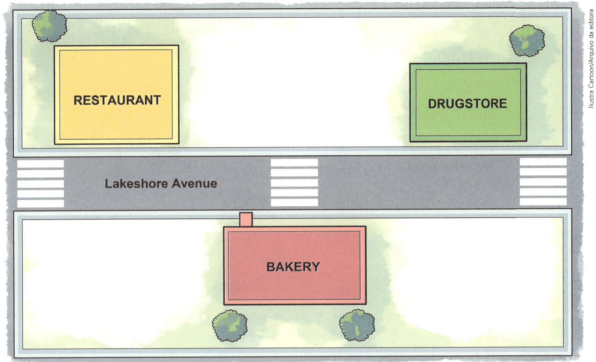

Lakeshore Avenue

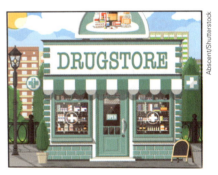

Restaurant .... Drugstore

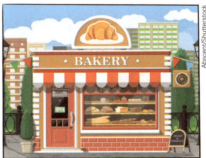

.... Bakery ....

3 Listen to the dialog and write **Yes** or **No**.

Let's go there!

A: Hi, Bob. Do you like Science museum?

B: Hi, Peter. Yes, the Science museum is cool, and it is next to the school.

A: That's great! Let's go to the museum.

B: Yes. But we need to buy the tickets.

A: No problem. I have two tickets.

B: O.K. Let's go.

a) ☐ The new museum is next to the shopping mall.

b) ☐ The boys need tickets to visit the museum.

c) ☐ The museum is next to the school.

4 Read and complete the sentences.

The Museum of Tomorrow (Museu do Amanhã) Admit one price $7 dollars.

Date: October 12, 2020.
Time: from 10:00 a.m. to: 5:00 p.m.

The Museum of Tomorrow is a new kind of museum. Visitors examine the past, learn about the current transformations in Science, explore future scenarios of a sustainable world and play interactive games in the museum.
Languages available: Portuguese, English and Spanish.
For the public the following services are available: cafeteria, restaurant and souvenir shops.

 Museu do **Amanhã**

a) The name of the museum in the picture is ....

....

b) It is located in ....

c) This is a .... museum.

d) There are .... games in the museum.

5 Write **T** (true) or **F** (false).

A museum ticket usually shows:

a) the admission fee of the museum.

b) the address of the museum.

c) the name of the museum.

d) your name on it.

e) the opening and closing time of the museum.

♪♫ **Let's Sing!**

Going to Places

🔊 Hi, Mom! Let's go to the amusement park.

(36) Yes, let's go! Yes, let's go!

So, Dad, let's go to the movie theater.

Yes, kids. Let's go!

Hip! Hip! Hooray!

Let's go!

Graham Oliver/Getty Images

TALKING ABOUT...

Saving Money!

E+/Getty Images

Pixel-Shot/Shutterstock

- What do these photos represent?
- Is money important?
- How do your parents or guardians get money?
- Why is it important to save money?

Diego Cerva/Shutterstock

I Believe I Can Fly/Shutterstock

1 Look, circle and count. Suppose you have

Vitaliy Gorban/Shutterstock

a)

Anna.zabella/Shutterstock

$ 5,00

b)

Natykach Nataliia/Shutterstock

$ 4,00

c)

SlipFloat/Shutterstock

$ 1,50

d)

MSSA/Shutterstock

$ 3,50

e)

Neonic Flower/Shutterstock

$ 2,50

f)

Kadzumo/Shutterstock

$ 3,00

FUN TIME

Join the Circle!

- Who are these people?
- What are they doing?
- Where are they?

-ᢓLet's Learn!ᢓ-

- Subject Pronouns
- Indoor and outdoor activities
- *It is a rainy day. Let's play indoors!*
- *It is a sunny day. Let's play outdoors!*

Fabiana Faiallo/Arquivo da editora

LET'S PLAY INDOORS

Listen and say

Key Words

1 Look, listen and say.

rainy day

sunny day

play cards

play video games

YOUR TURN TO PLAY, JONAH.

play board games

play chess

play mime games

watch cartoons

make cookies

Language Time

Subject Pronouns – Singular

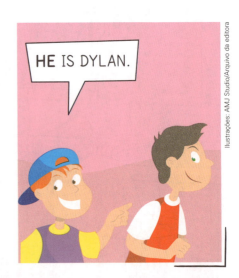

1 Complete the sentences with *I, you, he, she* or *it*.

a) .... am Daniel.

b) .... is my mother, Zoe.

c) .... is my father, William.

d) This is my bike. .... is red and new.

e) And .... are a student!

2 Read and complete with the missing letters.

a) ....ay b........................ games

b) pla................ ....ss

c) m............ke cook........................

d) w........................ cart................ns

3 Listen and make an X.

39

a)

Satria Tri Herwinantoko/Shutterstock

b)

Luigi650/Dreamstime/Glow Images

4 Break the code and write the message.

1	2	3	4	5	6	7	8	9	10	11	12	13	14	15	16
A	T	S	N	I	R	G	H	L	E	L	P	Y	D	O	C

5	2		3
		,	

6	1	5	4	13
				.

11	10	2		3
			,	

12	9	1	13

16	8	10	3	3

5	4	14	15	15	6	3	
							.

Now, We Know!

1 Match the columns and say.

a)

Werner Muenzker/ Shutterstock

watch cartoons

b)

syaochka/Shutterstock

play chess

c)

Kuki Ladron de Guevara/ Shutterstock

make cookies

d)

Realimage/Alamy/Fotoarena

play mime games

e)

BOOCYS/ Shutterstock

play cards

f)

Dmytro Zinkevych/Shutterstock

play board games

2 Find the missing part and answer. What kind of game is it?

It is a _____.

a)

b)

c)

d)

☐   ☐   ☐   ☐

3 Draw one indoor activity and write a sentence to describe it.

Let's Practice!

1 Answer and interview two classmates.

	YOU	Classmate # 1: (name: _____)	Classmate # 2: (name: _____)
What is your favorite indoor activity?			
What indoor activity is not your favorite?			
Write the name of one indoor activity you usually play, but it is not your favorite.			
What indoor activity your friends play?			
What indoor activity you dislike?			

2 Practice the questions and the answers. Use the words from the box.

> **play cards**   **play video games**   **play board games**
> **play mime games**   **make cookies**   **watch cartoons**

WHAT IS THE WEATHER LIKE TODAY?

IT IS RAINY TODAY. LET'S PLAY AN INDOOR GAME!

BlueRingMedia/Shutterstock

I WANT TO ....

3 Talk to a classmate about rules for playing games.

Are they necessary? Yes./No.

Why?

4 Read the sentences and write YES or NO.

a) It is important to define the rules to play games. ....

b) Rules are not important when we play games. ....

5 Read the conversation and answer: In your opinion, are they having fun or arguing with each other? What can help them stop it and play fair?

LET'S PLAY A GAME. FIRST, WE NEED TO DEFINE THE RULES.

WHY IS IT IMPORTANT TO HAVE RULES, TOM?

BECAUSE IT HELPS US TO PLAY FAIR.

RULES ARE IMPORTANT TO AVOID ARGUMENTS AND CHEATING.

SO LET'S WRITE OUR RULES NOW.

Sirayama/Arquivo da editora

6 Read the checkers game rules.

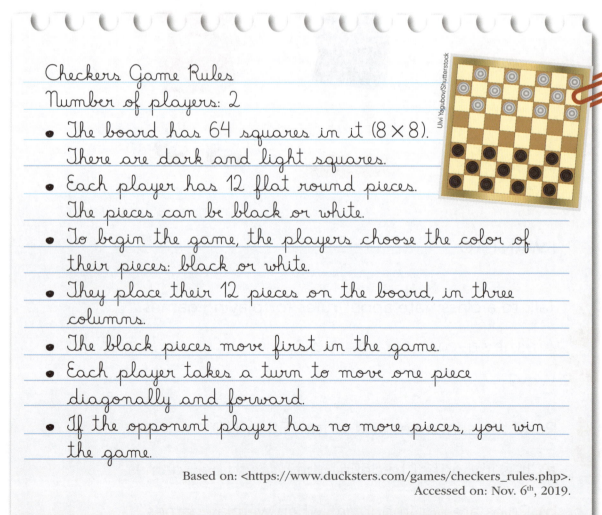

Ulvi Yagubov/Shutterstock

Checkers Game Rules

Number of players: 2

- The board has 64 squares in it (8 × 8). There are dark and light squares.
- Each player has 12 flat round pieces. The pieces can be black or white.
- To begin the game, the players choose the color of their pieces: black or white.
- They place their 12 pieces on the board, in three columns.
- The black pieces move first in the game.
- Each player takes a turn to move one piece diagonally and forward.
- If the opponent player has no more pieces, you win the game.

Based on: <https://www.ducksters.com/games/checkers_rules.php>.
Accessed on: Nov. 6th, 2019.

7 Read the text and circle the correct answers.

a) What is the name of the game?

checkers   chess   card game

b) How many players participate?

10   2   64

c) What kind of material is needed to play this game?

a board and black and white pieces

a board and red and blue markers

a set of cards and a board game

d) Which player plays the first move?

white pieces player   black pieces player

8 Talk to your classmates. Ask and answer.

a) Are rules important to play games in a fair way? Why?

b) After reading the rules, did you learn anything new or different about this game? What?

🎵♪ Let's Sing!

Let's play indoors today!

It's raining!	And also video games.
It's raining!	Board games, mime games,
So let's play indoors!	And also video games.
So let's play indoors!	Let's have some fun!
Board games, mime games,	Let's have some fun!

LET'S PLAY OUTDOORS

Listen and say

41

Key Words

1 Look, listen and say.

42

sunny and warm

cloudy

cold

play dodgeball

play basketball

hide-and-seek

ride a bike

jump rope

Subject Pronouns – Plural

WE ARE BEST FRIENDS.

YOU ARE SALLY AND PAUL.

THEY ARE DANIEL AND KIM.

Ilustrações: Sirayama/Arquivo da editora

1 Complete the sentences with *I, You, She, It, We, They*.

a) .... am a good basketball player.

Ljupco Smokovski/Shutterstock

b) .... are best friends.

Lopolo/Shutterstock

c) .... are soccer players.

Tetra images RF/Getty Images

d) .... is an ice cream.

futuristman/Shutterstock

e) .... is a Math teacher.

Rido/Shutterstock

f) .... are dodgeball players.

Fernando Favoretto/Criar Imagem

2 Read and complete the answers. What is the weather like in each picture?

| rainy | sunny | cloudy | cold |

a) It is a _____ day.

aarrows/Shutterstock

b) It is a _____ day.

Serg64/Shutterstock

c) It is a _____ day.

Vereshchagin Dmitry/Shutterstock

d) It is a _____ day.

Ricardo Valerio Sanches/Shutterstock

3 Write the name of four outdoor games using only the letters below.

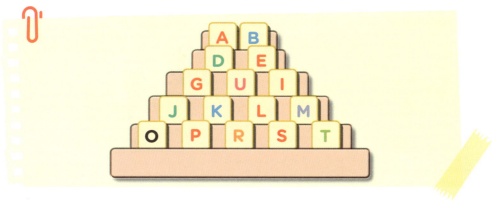

....

....

Now, We Know!

1 Complete the sequence and write the name of the missing one.

a)

....

b)

....

c)

....

d)

....

2 Unscramble the words to make sentences.

a) a / sunny / day / It / is / ....

b) school / is / he / at / ....

c) is / she / mother / my / ....

d) student / a / are / you / ....

e) bike / my / blue / is / ....

3 Listen and find the way.

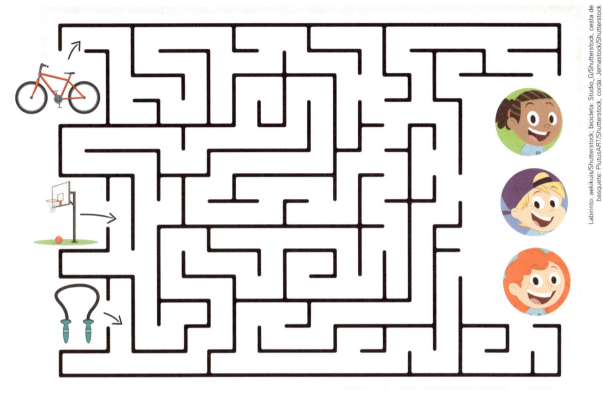

4 Write *he, she, it*.

a) a schoolbag - ___it___

b) a boy - _____

c) a girl - _____

d) a dog – _____

Let's Practice!

1 Play tic-tac-toe.

1	2	3
4	5	6
7	8	9

1. It is a sunny day. Let's play...

....

2. It is a rainy day. Let's play...

....

3. It is a cold day. Let's play...

....

4. What is your favorite kind of weather?

....

5. What is your favorite indoor activity?

....

6. What is your favorite outdoor activity?

....

7. Write the name of two indoor activities.

....

....

8. Write the name of two outdoor activities.

....

....

9. Give one example of other outdoor or indoor activity you do.

....

BlueRingMedia/Shutterstock

2 List the activities mentioned in the correct column.

Favorite indoor activities 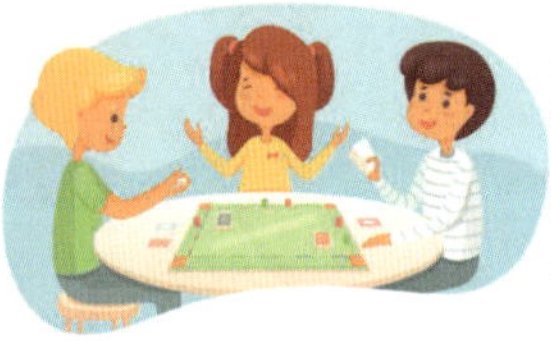	Favorite outdoor activities 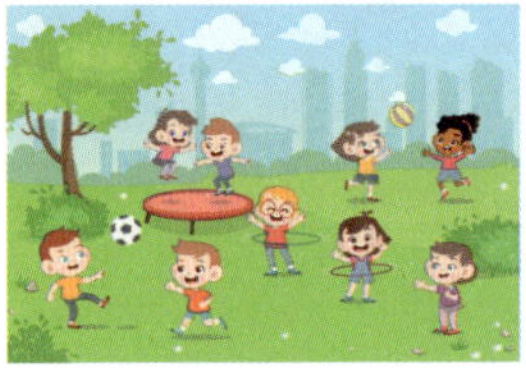	Favorite kind of weather 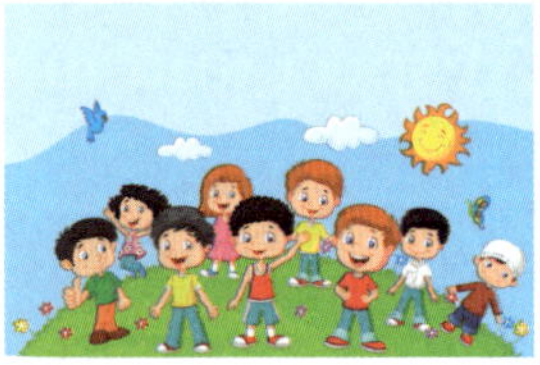

3 Read and make an **X**.

a) Indoor activities are

☐ board games.   ☐ cooking.

☐ crafts.   ☐ volleyball.

b) Outdoor activities are

☐ basketball.   ☐ hide-and-seek.

☐ picnic.   ☐ watch cartoons.

c) Fair play is related to

☐ respect.   ☐ being kind.

☐ help each other.   ☐ disrespecting rules.

4 Read the text and write **T** (true) or **F** (false).

Playing Fair

Playing fair is related to respect and making choices in a game. When we interact with each other during a game, we must consider what we think is right and what is not.

Fair Play Players should:
- **Know and understand** the rules before the game.
- Play fair based on the game **rules**.
- Keep **emotions** under control.
- **Respect** their opponent team.
- Be **honest** and **kind**.
- **Help** each other.
- **Learn** from each other.

Based on: <https://oakvillelittleleague.com/?page_id=476>. Accessed on: Nov. 6th, 2019.

In fair play...

a) rules are not important.

b) being kind is relevant.

c) it is necessary to understand the rules before the game.

d) it is not important to be honest and help each other.

e) respect all players.

5 Break the code!

A	I	Y	F	L	P	R
❤	✳	◆	❑	▲	✕	○

✕	▲	❤	◆		❑	❤	✳	○	
P	L	A	Y		F	A	I	R	!

In groups, write a sentence about "fair play".

 **Let's Sing!**

Fair Play Song

44

Be respectful!

Be kind!

Be honest!

Be fair!

Playing fairly and having fun.

It's more important than winning.

Always do the right thing,

Under any circumstances.

Respect the rules,

And follow them!

Equal chances for everyone!

It's fair play! It's fair play!

OSTILL is Franck Camhi/Shutterstock

IT'S YOUR TURN!

Let's Make a Checkerboard!

 Follow the steps below.

YOU NEED:

- cardboard from a box (30 cm × × 30 m × 2 cm)

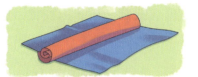
- colored paper (any color) to cover the cardboard

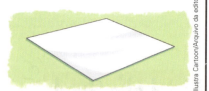
- white cardboard (24 cm × 24 cm)

- 12 circles in black cardboard to cover the top of the PET bottle caps

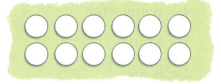
- 12 circles in white cardboard to cover the top of the PET bottle caps

- 12 PET bottle caps covered with black cardboard

- 12 PET bottle caps covered with white cardboard

- a pencil, a ruler, an eraser, a pair of scissors and glue

- black crayon or markers

Ilustra Cartoon/Arquivo da editora

How to make it:

Step 1: Cut a piece of cardboard from an empty box (size: 30 cm × 30 cm × 2 cm).

Step 2: Cover the cardboard base using the colored paper.

Step 3: Cut a square piece of white cardboard (size: 24 cm × 24 cm).

Step 4: Draw the grid of the board. Each square must be 3 cm × 3 cm.

Step 5: Paint the squares black to make the chess (paint one and skip the next one).

Step 6: Glue the grid on the middle of the cardboard base. Leave a margin of 3 cm using a ruler and a pencil.

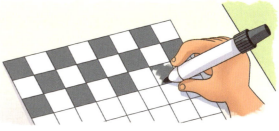

Step 7: Glue the black and white tops on the bottle caps. Then put them on the board and have fun.

Based on: <https://www.womansday.com/home/crafts-projects/
how-to/a5749/craft-how-to-checkerboard-118728/>
Accessed on: October 29th, 2019.

Ilustra Cartoon/Arquivo da editora.

1 Read and make an **X**.

a) My mother's sister is my...

☐ aunt.   ☐ sister.   ☐ uncle.

b) My mother's mother is my...

☐ aunt.   ☐ sister.   ☐ grandma.

c) My father's son is my...

☐ uncle.   ☐ brother.   ☐ grandpa.

d) My dad's brother is my...

☐ uncle.   ☐ aunt.   ☐ grandpa.

2 Read and draw the family tree.

> Hi, my name is George. My dad's name is Lucius, my mother is Gina, my baby brother is Ben and I have two sisters – Sara and Sally.

REVIEW →→ It's Ten O'clock

1 Write the sentences from the box in the correct place.

> It's eight o'clock. Good morning! / It's ten o'clock.
> Good night! / It's six o'clock. Good evening!
> / It's three o'clock. Good afternoon!

kryzhov/Shutterstock

....

....

Vergani Fotografia/Shutterstock

....

....

Tony Tallec/Caiaimage/Fotoarena

....

....

Evgeny Atamanenko/Shutterstock

....

....

REVIEW → A Special Day at School

1 Write the days of the week.

| **What do they do in the afternoon?** |

a) On M ....

b) On T ....

c) On W ....

d) On Th ....

e) On F ....

f) On S ....

g) On S ....

REVIEW Be Nice!

1 Write the missing letters.

a) This is a s_____p_____rm_____rk_____t.

b) This is a sch_____l.

c) This is a p_____rk.

d) This is a m _____s_____m.

e) This is a sp_____rts cl_____b.

f) This is a sh_____pp_____ng m_____ll.

➔➔➔ **It's Time for Lunch!**

1 Find, circle and write food and drink words.

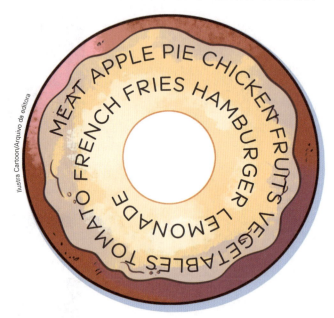

MEAT APPLE PIE CHICKEN FRUITS HAMBURGER VEGETABLES LEMONADE TOMATO FRENCH FRIES

Ilustra Cartoon/Arquivo da editora

....

....

....

....

....

....

....

....

2 Write the plural forms.

a)

Milagr/Shutterstock

....

b)

BlueRingMedia/Shutterstock

....

c)

Paullaparaula/Shutterstock

....

d)

Innochka/Shutterstock

....

Places in the City

1 Find the way and write.

....

....

....

....

1 Write the pronouns **I**, **he**, **she**, **it**, **you**.

a) This is Millie. .... is my sister.

b) This is Daniel. .... is my friend.

c) This is Buddy. .... is my dog.

d) Look at that cat. .... is black.

e) This present is for ...., Tom. Happy birthday!

f) .... am a student.

2 Complete the sentences using the words from the box.

outdoors	indoors	cake	board	today	cartoons

a) It is a rainy day. Let's play ....!

b) It is a sunny day. Let's play ....!

c) What is the weather like ....?

d) You can play a .... game, a video game or a mime game.

e) Let's watch ....

f) Let's make a ....!

3 Answer the questions.

a) What is your favorite indoor activity? It is ....

b) What is the weather like today? It is ....

Let's Play Outdoors

1 Write the pronouns **we**, **you**, **they**.

a) Emily, Agatha and Bill are friends. .... are very

good friends.

b) Vivian, Valerie and I are in the same basketball team.

.... are school friends.

c) Bill, Bob and I are in the same classroom at school.

.... are in Class B.

d) This is Snow and that is Buddy. .... are dogs.

e) These board games are presents for ....,

children! Have fun!

2 Unscramble the words about outdoor activities.

a) gedodllab   ....

b) babastekll   ....

c) pmuj epor   ....

d) edhi-dan-kees   ....

e) edir a kbie   ....

3 Complete the sentences.

a) My favorite outdoor activity is ....

b) Today is ....

→ **My Family**

1 Draw your family tree and write their names.

....

....

....

....

....

1 Break the code to find the time. Draw the clock hands.

A	B	C	D	E	F	G	H	I	J	K	L	M
♥	✠	✽	☛	✳	🐛	♦	✿	✵	➡	❋	✈	☯

N	O	P	Q	R	S	T	U	V	W	X	Y	Z
◻	▷	✌	✳	†	☎	✉	◍	✸	➤	☺	✎	◈

T

a) It's .... o'clock.

b) It's ....o'clock.

c) It's .... o'clock.

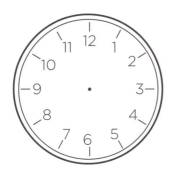

d) It's .... o'clock.

1 Crossword. Write the numbers.

```
                    18        17         0
                              S          Z
         19                   E          E  R  O
                              V          R        9
         3   T  H  R  E  E    N     1    O
                              T
                    2         E
                              E
                              E
              13
         20  T  W  E  N  T  Y             16
                                    7
         8   E  I  G  H  T      6    S  E  V  E  N
                                    E
                    14       4     V
              15              F     E  N
                              O
                              U     12
                              R
                  11    E  L  E  V  E
         5   F  I  V  E
                       10   T  E
```

1 Search and write.

✦(A)	✳(B)	✿(C)	✺(D)	◈(E)	✴(H)	♥(I)	❄(K)
A	B	C	D	E	H	I	K

✍(L)	◻(N)	❋(O)	◎(P)	💣(R)	✋(S)	☎(T)	✦(U)
L	N	O	P	R	S	T	U

◈	💣	✦	✋	◈	💣

◻	❋	☎	◈	✳	❋	❋	❄

✳	❋	✦	💣	✺

✺	◈	✋	❄

LET'S PLAY! → **It's Time for Lunch!**

1 Color and write.

Ilustra Cartoon/Arquivo da editora

1) ....

2) ....

3) ....

4) ....

5) ....

6) ....

LET'S PLAY! → Places in the City

1 Look and complete the sentences.

a) The amusement park is next to the ....

b) The museum is between ....

and ....

c) The blue house is next to the ....

d) The .... is in front of the restaurant.

e) The .... is between the pet

shop and the bakery.

Parque: BlueRingMedia/Shutterstock; teatro: Tetsuo Buseteru/Shutterstock; museu: Abscent/Shutterstock; farmácia: Abscent/Shutterstock; padaria: Abscent/ Shutterstock; cinema: Vector Tradition/Shutterstock; petshop: BigMouse/Shutterstock; casas: Banco de imagens/Arquivo da editora; restaurante: DRogatnev/Shutterstock.

LET'S PLAY! → Let's Play Indoors

1 Complete the puzzle. Then find the mystery sentence.

a)

P		A	Y	*	C	A	R	D	S

b)

W	A	T	C	H	*	C		R	T	O	O	N	S

c)

P	L	A		*	V	I	D	E	O	*	G	A		E

d)

M	A	K	E	*	C	O	O	K		E	S

e)

P	L	A	Y	*	B	O	A	R	D	*	G	A		

f)

P	L		Y	*	C	H	E	S	S

g)

P	L	A	Y	*	C	H		C	K	E	R	S

The mystery sentence is...

	a	b	c		c	d	e			f		g
P			*					*	G	M		

LET'S PLAY! ➤ Let's Play Outdoors

brgfx/Shutterstock

1 Look at the pictures, find and circle the words. Write the actions.

D	Q	Y	Y	R	M	T	R	Q	G	R	U	Y
O	D	M	N	U	B	A	S	U	O	I	S	Z
D	S	A	M	I	Z	F	B	X	I	D	F	D
G	V	J	U	M	P	*	R	O	P	E	D	T
E	Z	X	A	O	C	Y	H	E	W	*	F	O
B	A	S	K	E	T	B	A	L	L	A	G	R
A	C	Z	T	H	L	D	U	T	X	*	B	N
L	X	W	E	R	F	V	C	U	O	B	A	O
L	Y	H	Y	D	I	X	G	Y	V	I	M	A
K	U	B	F	J	K	P	Q	A	E	K	U	T
H	I	D	E	-	A	N	D	-	S	E	E	K

a) ....

b) ....

c) ....

d) ....

e) ....

Victor Brave/Shutterstock

brgfx/Shutterstock

Lorelyn Medina/Shutterstock

BlueRingMedia/Shutterstock

one hundred and nineteen **119**

AUDIO TRANSCRIPT

Track 3

a) Steve is my father.

b) Annie is my mother.

c) Noah is my brother.

d) Corine is my grandma.

e) Ivan is my grandpa.

f) Lily is my sister.

Track 5

What color is flower number 1? It is orange.

What color is flower number 2? It is pink.

What color is flower number 3? It is yellow.

What color is flower number 4? It is red.

What color is flower number 5? It is blue.

Track 6

1. This is my mother, Annie. Nice to meet you, Annie.

2. This is my father, Steve. Nice to meet you, Steve.

3. This is my grandpa, Ivan. Nice to meet you, Ivan.

4. This is my grandma, Corine. Nice to meet you, Corine.

Track 10

1. Good morning!

2. Good afternoon!

3. Good evening!

4. Good night!

Track 11

a) It's four o'clock.

b) It's six o'clock.

c) It's three o'clock.

d) It's seven o'clock.

e) It's one o'clock.

f) It's eleven o'clock.

Track 18

On Mondays, Emily goes to school by school bus.

On Tuesdays, Emily goes to school by bike.

On Wednesdays, Emily goes to school by subway.

On Thursdays, Emily goes to school by train.

On Fridays, Emily goes to school by car.

Track 23

a) a student   **b)** a classroom   **c)** an eraser   **d)** a notebook   **e)** a chair

Track 24

1. a tall student

2. a big pencil

3. a short student

4. a small pencil

Track 33

1. Good morning! Bread and milk, please.

2. For me, rice and beans, chicken and lemonade, please.

3. Let's check my shopping list. I need some vegetables and fruit.

4. What a beautiful blue bird!

Track 34

a) The amusement park is between the restaurant and the drugstore.

b) The museum is in front of the restaurant.

c) The pet shop is next to the bakery.

Track 39

Today is not a sunny day. It is a rainy day.

Peter is not playing outdoors. He is sad.

Track 43

Lily: Let's play outdoors. I love jumping rope.

Tom: And I love to ride my bike. It is fun!

Millie: I prefer to play basketball. It is cool!

GLOSSARY

A

a: um, uma
about: sobre
according to: de acordo com
activity: atividade
admission fee: preço da entrada
admit: admitir
always: sempre
all: tudo, todos
am: sou; estou
amusement park: parque de diversões

an: um, uma
and: e
answer: resposta; responder
anything: alguma coisa
apple: maçã
apple juice: suco de maçã
apple pie: torta de maçã
are: são; estão
argue: brigar, discutir
argument: discussão
art museum: museu de arte
ask: perguntar; pedir
at: no, na, para
attention: atenção
Australia: Austrália
available: disponível
avoid: evitar

B

bakery: padaria

ball: bola
balloon: bexiga, balão
bank: banco
basketball: basquetebol
bat: morcego
be fair: ser justo
be honest: ser honesto
be kind: ser generoso
be nice: seja bom, seja legal
be respectful: ser respeitoso
be rude: ser mal-educado, grosseiro
beach: praia
beans: feijões
beautiful: bonito
before: antes
begin: começar
best friend: melhor amigo
between: entre
big: grande
bike: bicicleta
black: preto
blackbird: pássaro-preto
blue: azul
board: lousa, tabuleiro (de jogo)
board game: jogo de tabuleiro
boat: barco
body: corpo
book: livro
box: caixa
boy: menino
break the code: decifrar a mensagem
breakfast: café da manhã
brother: irmão
brown: marrom
bus: ônibus
but: mas
buy: comprar
bye-bye: tchau; até logo

C

cafeteria: cantina
can: pode
can't: não pode
Canada: Canadá
car: carro

cardboard: cartolina, papelão
cardboard box: caixa de papelão
cat: gato
chair: cadeira

Codrut Crososchi/Shutterstock

character: personagem
cheat: enganar, trapacear
check: verificar
checkers: jogo de damas
checkerboard: tabuleiro de jogo de damas
cheese: queijo
chess: xadrez
chicken: frango
children: crianças
choose: escolher
circle: circular, círculo
circumstances: circunstâncias
city: cidade
classmate: colega de turma
classroom: sala de aula
clock: relógio
clock hand: ponteiro de relógio
closing time: horário de fechamento
clothing buttons: botões de roupa
cloud: nuvem
cloudy: nublado
coffee: café
cold: frio
color: cor; colorir
colored: colorido
colored pens: canetas coloridas
column: coluna
comic strip: história em quadrinhos
complete: completar
cookies: biscoitos

cooking: arte culinária
count: contar
countries: países
countryside: campo, área rural
cover: cobrir
craft: artesanato
create: criar
crepe paper: papel crepom
crossword: palavras cruzadas
current: atual
cut: cortar
cute: gracioso, bonito, fofo

D

dad: papai
dangerous: perigoso
dark: escuro
date: data
daughter: filha
day: dia
day by day: dia após dia, diariamente
deadline: prazo
define: definir
delicious: delicioso
desk: carteira escolar

Edilus/Shutterstock

diagonally: diagonalmente
dinner: jantar
dislike: não gostar
do: fazer
doesn't: não (negação com verbo auxiliar, 3ª pessoa do singular)
dodgeball: queimada

Lorelyn Medina/Shutterstock

dog: cachorro
doll: boneca
don't: não (negação com verbo auxiliar)
door: porta
draw: desenhar
drink: beber
drugstore: farmácia

Abscent/Shutterstock

E

eat: comer
egg: ovo
eight: oito
eighteen: dezoito
eleven: onze
emotions: emoções, sentimentos
empty: vazio
England: Inglaterra
English: inglês
eraser: borracha de apagar
everyone: todos, todo mundo
example: exemplo
experiment: experiência, experimento

F

fair: justo
fair play: jogo limpo, justo, sem trapaças
fair way: forma justa
false: falso
family: família
family tree: árvore genealógica
father: pai
fifteen: quinze
fifty: cinquenta
find: achar, encontrar
first: primeiro
five: cinco
floor: chão
flower: flor
follow: seguir
for: para
for fun: por diversão
forty: quarenta
forty-eight: quarenta e oito
forty-five: quarenta e cinco
forty-four: quarenta e quatro
forty-nine: quarenta e nove
forty-one: quarenta e um
forty-seven: quarenta e sete

forty-six: quarenta e seis
forty-three: quarenta e três
forty-two: quarenta e dois
forward: adiante, para a frente
four: quatro
fourteen: catorze, quatorze
French fries: batatas fritas
Friday: sexta-feira
friend: amigo(a)
frog: rã
from: de
fruit: fruta
fun: diversão

G

game: jogo
gap: lacuna
garden: jardim, horta
get: pegar, conseguir
girl: menina, garota
give: dar
glass: vidro; copo
glue: colar; cola
go: ir
going: indo
gold: ouro
good: bom
good afternoon: boa tarde
good evening: boa noite
good morning: bom dia
goodbye: até logo, tchau
good night: boa noite (na hora de dormir)
grandfather: avô
grandma: vovó
grandmother: avó
grandpa: vovô
grass: grama
gray: cinza (cor)
great: grande; ótimo
great idea!: boa ideia!
green: verde
greetings: saudações
grid: tabela, grade
guardians: responsáveis, guardiões
guess: adivinhar
guy: cara

H

ham: presunto
happy: feliz
have: ter

he: ele
healthy food: alimento saudável
helicopter: helicóptero
hello: olá, alô
help: ajudar; ajuda
help each other: ajudar uns aos outros
here: aqui
hi: oi
hide-and-seek: esconde--esconde

his: seu, dele
home: lar
homework: tarefa de casa
horse: cavalo
house: casa
how: como
how cute!: que lindo!
how many...?: Quanto...?
Hurray!: Viva!

I

i: eu
I'm: eu sou; eu estou
ice cream: sorvete de massa
improve: melhorar
in: em, dentro
in front of: em frente a
indoor: interior, interno
interactive: interativo
interview: entrevistar; entrevista
is: é; está
it: ele, ela (animais e objetos)

J

job: trabalho
joke: brincar, brincadeira
juice: suco

jump rope: corda, pular corda

June: junho
junk food: comida sem valor nutritivo

K

keep: manter(-se)
kid: criança
know: saber; conhecer

L

lake: lago
laminated paper: papel laminado
lamppost: poste de luz
language: idioma
learn: aprender
left: esquerdo
lemonade: limonada
let's: vamos
let's play: vamos jogar, brincar
letters: letras
light: claro, luz
like: gostar
located: localizado
listen: escutar, ouvir
look: olhar
love: amor; amar
lovely: belo, agradável
lunch: almoço

M

make: fazer
make cookies: fazer biscoitos
mall: *shopping center*
many: muitos
map: mapa
marker: marcador
match: ligar, relacionar
Math: Matemática
May: maio
me: me, mim
meal: comida, refeição
means of transportation: meios de transporte

meat: carne
message: mensagem
middle: meio
milk: leite
mime game: jogo de mímica
miss: sentir falta de
mobility: mobilidade
model: modelo, maquete
mom: mamãe
mommy: mamãe
Monday: segunda-feira
money: dinheiro
moon: lua
morning: manhã
mother: mãe
motorcycle: motocicleta, moto
mouse: camundongo, *mouse* de computador
move: mover
movie theater: cinema
ms.: senhorita
museum: museu
my: meu, minha

N

name: nome
need: precisar
new: novo
next one: próximo
next to: próximo a
nice: bom, agradável, legal
nigerian: nigeriano
night: noite
nine: nove
nineteen: dezenove
no: não
nose: nariz
not: não
note: anotação
notebook: caderno
now: agora
number: número; numerar

O

o'clock: hora exata
odd: estranho
of: de
old: velho
on: em, sobre
one: um
only: apenas, somente

opening time: horário de abertura
opponent: oponente, adversário
orange: laranja
our: nosso, nossa
outdoor: exterior, ao ar live

P

packaging: embalagem
page: página
paint: pintar
parents: pais
park: parque
past: passado
pay: pagar
pen: caneta
pencil: lápis
pencil case: estojo
pencil sharpener: apontador de lápis

Laurentiu Timplaru/ Shutterstock

people: pessoas
pet: animal de estimação
PET bottle cap: tampinha de garrafa plástica
photo: fotografia
picnic: piquenique
picture: figura, fotografia
pie: torta
pieces: peças
pink: cor-de-rosa
place: lugar
plane: avião
plastic: plástico
play: brincar; jogar; tocar
play fair: fazer algo de maneira justa e honesta
player: jogador
please: por favor
polite words: palavras educadas
Portuguese: português
preposition: preposição
price: preço
profile: perfil
purple: roxo
put: pôr

R

rain: chuva; chover
rainbow: arco-íris
raining: chovendo
rainy day: dia chuvoso

Iconic Bestiary/Shutterstock

red: vermelho
respect: respeito; respeitar
rice: arroz
ride a bike: andar de bicicleta
right: direito; certo
rollerblades: patins com uma fileira de rodinhas

cosmaa/Shutterstock

ruler: régua
rule: regra

S

sad: triste
safe: seguro; protegido
salad: salada
sandwich: sanduíche
Saturday: sábado
sausage: salsicha, linguiça
save: poupar
say: dizer
scenery: cenário, paisagem
school: escola
school bus: ônibus escolar

Ilustra Cartoon/ Arquivo da editora

school objects: objetos escolares
schoolbag: mochila escolar
Science: ciências
scissors: tesoura
scooter: lambreta, patinete
sea: mar
search: procurar
see: ver
sentence: sentença
service: serviço
seven: sete
seventeen: dezessete
she: ela
ship: navio
shopping list: lista de compras
shopping mall: *shopping center*
short: baixo; curto
should: deve
show: mostrar
sing: cantar
sister: irmã
sit: sentar-se
six: seis
sixteen: dezesseis
skateboard: *skate*, esqueite
skip: pular
sky: céu
sleep: dormir
small: pequeno
so: assim; então
soccer: futebol
soccer player: jogador de futebol
some: algum, alguns, um pouco de
son: filho
sorry: desculpe(-me)
souvenirs shop: loja de lembrancinhas
Spanish: espanhol
square: quadrado
star: estrela
start: começar
step: passo, etapa
stick: colar
stop: parar
street: rua
student: estudante, aluno
subject: disciplina escolar
subway: metrô
sun: sol
Sunday: domingo

sunny day: dia ensolarado

supermarket: supermercado
sustainable: sustentável
swim: nadar

T

take a turn: vez de jogar
talk: conversa; falar
tall: alto
teacher: professor
ten: dez
thanks: obrigado (obrigada)
that: aquele, aquela, aquilo
the: o, a, os, as
the United States: os Estados Unidos
theater: teatro
there: lá
they: eles, elas
these: estes, estas
thin: magro
thing: coisa
thirteen: treze
thirty: trinta
thirty-eight: trinta e oito
thirty-five: trinta e cinco
thirty-four: trinta e quatro
thirty-nine: trinta e nove
thirty-one: trinta e um
thirty-seven: trinta e sete
thirty-six: trinta e seis
thirty-three: trinta e três
thirty-two: trinta e dois
this: este, esta, isto
three: três
through: através de, por
Thursday: quinta-feira
ticket: bilhete, ingresso
Tic-tac-toe: jogo da velha
time: hora
to: para

today: hoje
tomato: tomate
tomorrow: amanhã
too: demasiado, muito; também
toy: brinquedo
tractor: trator
traffic light: semáforo
train: trem
tree: árvore

truck: caminhão
true: verdadeiro
Tuesday: terça-feira
turn: virar
twelve: doze
twenty: vinte
twenty-eight: vinte e oito
twenty-five: vinte e cinco
twenty-four: vinte e quatro
twenty-nine: vinte e nove
twenty-one: vinte e um
twenty-seven: vinte e sete
twenty-six: vinte e seis
twenty-three: vinte e três
twenty-two: vinte e dois
two: dois, duas

U

ugly: feio
under: sob, embaixo de
under control: sob controle
underground: metrô
understand: compreender
unscramble: desembaralhar
unhealthy: não saudável
use: usar
usually: geralmente

V

vegetables: legumes

very: muito
violet: violeta
visitor: visitante

W

wake up: despertar
want: querer
watch cartoons: assistir a desenhos animados
water: água
way: caminho; modo
we: nós
weather: tempo, clima
Wednesday: quarta-feira
week: semana
weekend: fim de semana
welcome: bem-vindo
what: que, qual, o que, o qual
wheels: rodas
when: quando
where: onde
white: branco
who: quem
why: por quê?
window: janela
with: com
woman: mulher
woof, woof: au, au (latido)
word: palavra
world: mundo
worry: preocupar-se
write: escrever

Y

years old: idade
yellow: amarelo
yes: sim
you: você, vocês
your: seu(s), sua(s)
you're welcome: de nada, por nada (resposta que se dá a alguém que acabou de agradecer por algo).

Z

zero: zero

Books

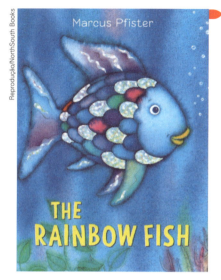

Reprodução/NorthSouth Books

Marcus Pfister. English Translation: J. Alison James. **The Rainbow Fish**. North-South Books; Edição: Later Printing, 1999.

O peixinho Rainbow Fish percebe que ser o peixe mais bonito do mar pode ser solitário, então ele descobre que há mais a ganhar compartilhando suas qualidades especiais do que mantendo-as todas para si.

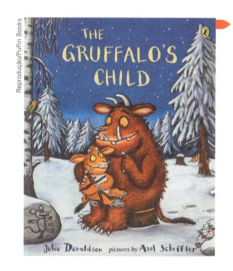

Reprodução/Puffin Books

Julia Donaldson. Illustrations: Axel Sheffler. **The Gruffalo's Child**. Puffin Books; Edição: Reprint, 2007.

Esta é a história do filho de Gruffalo que, apesar do aviso do pai, parte em direção à floresta escura para encontrar o "rato grande e ruim", a única coisa de que seu pai tem medo.

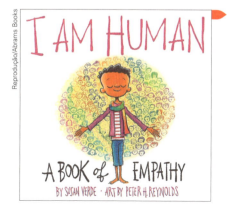

Reprodução/Abrams Books

Susan Verde. Illustrations: Peter H. Reynolds. **I Am Human**: A Book of Empathy.; Edição: Harry N. Abrams, 2018.

Esta história retrata o que significa ser humano e viver em um mundo desafiador e cheio de emoções. **I Am Human** mostra que nós, seres humanos, cometemos erros e podemos fazer boas escolhas na vida, seja por meio de um sorriso, seja pelo uso de palavras de cortesia ou mesmo um pedido de desculpas. Este livro é uma celebração de empatia e encoraja o ser humano a dar sempre seu melhor.

● Sites

http://www.primarygames.com/#

Este *site* traz jogos interativos de temáticas variadas como: culinária, esportes, aventura e muitas outras. Nele também é possível montar quebra-cabeças, selecionar jogos que desafiam o raciocínio lógico, além de aprender Matemática, Ciências, Estudos Sociais e desenvolver a leitura.

https://pbskids.org/

PBS Kids disponibiliza mais de 230 jogos interativos, classificados em *popular games*, *hard games*, *new games*, *feeling games*, *teamwork games*, *adventure games*, entre outros.

https://joysunbear.com/play-and-learn/

Esta é uma página divertida para crianças. Nela, poderão aprender sobre Joy, seus amigos e suas viagens ao redor do mundo, além de fazer *download* de atividades para colorir e de jogos de diferentes lugares do planeta.

Acesso em: nov. 2019.

BIBLIOGRAPHY

ALMEIDA FILHO, J. C. P. *Dimensões comunicativas no ensino de línguas*. 2. ed. Campinas: Pontes, 2000.

BRASIL. Base Nacional Comum Curricular (BNCC). Brasília: MEC, 2018. Disponível em: <http://base nacionalcomum.mec.gov.br/>. Acesso em: 26 set. 2019.

CELANI, M. A. A. *Ensino de segunda língua*: redescobrindo as origens. São Paulo: Educ, 1997.

HARMER, J. *The Practice of English Language Teaching*. 4. ed. London: Pearson Longman, 2007.

MOITA LOPES, L. P. A nova ordem mundial, os Parâmetros Curriculares Nacionais e o ensino de inglês no Brasil. A base intelectual para uma ação política. In: BARBARA, L.; RAMOS, R. de C. G. *Reflexão e ações no ensino-aprendizagem de línguas*. São Paulo: Mercado de Letras, 2003.

VYGOTSKY, L. S. *A formação social da mente*: o desenvolvimento dos processos psicológicos superiores. São Paulo: Martins Fontes, 1991.

TIC-TAC-TOE

Score

Siriyama/Arquivo da editora

Rosto: Banco de imagens/Arquivo da editora, ovo frito e salsichas: Sirayama/Arquivo da editora; sanduíche: Anna.zabella/Shutterstock

Suco de caixa, bife, salada e frango: Siriyama/Arquivo da editora; batata frita: MSSA/Shutterstock, suco de garrafa: Neonic Flower/Shutterstock; torta: Paulaparaula/Shutterstock

STICKERS

🔴 Lesson 1 My Family

Ilustrações: Siriyama/Arquivo da editora

🔴 Lesson 2 It's Ten O'clock

AlinaMD/Shutterstock

LiiKar/Shutterstock

M. Pellinni/Shutterstock

BlackSnake/Shutterstock

Balazs Kovacs/Shutterstock

Jaroslav Bartoš/Shutterstock

Serg64/Shutterstock

Suppaki|1017/Shutterstock

psoundphoto/Shutterstock

Paul Orr/Shutterstock

Vladitto/Shutterstock

Ozerov Alexander/Shutterstock

Banana Republic images/Shutterstock

filmfoto/Shutterstock

saiva/Shutterstock

Banco de imagens/
Arquivo da editora

❤ Lesson 3 A Special Day at School

omnimoney/Shutterstock

Verko_o/Shutterstock

inkwellapp/Shutterstock

cosmaa/Shutterstock

akud/Shutterstock

ghrzuzudu/Shutterstock

Svetlana Kutsyn/Shutterstock

Matheus Obst/Shutterstock

Where is Noah?

Eliete Canesi Morino
Rita Brugin de Faria

Aluno: ....

Escola: .... Turma: ....

editora scipione